B.C. TRUCKIN ON DOWN

by
Johnny Hart

FAWCETT GOLD MEDAL • NEW YORK

B.C./TRUCKIN ON DOWN

11-14

SPROING

11-18

THAT'S WHATCHA
CALL ONE OF YOUR
TONGUE-IN-CHEEK
ANTEATERS.

11-19

11·21

HOP ON,..I'LL TAKE YOU TO A NIFTY HIDING PLACE TILL AFTER THANKSGIVING!
OH, THANK YOU!
I'LL NEVER UNDERSTAND WHY TURTLES CAN FLY, AND TURKEYS CAN'T!
*BUT I THOUGHT YOU.....
...ME AND MY BIG BEAK!
11-25

12·1

12·3

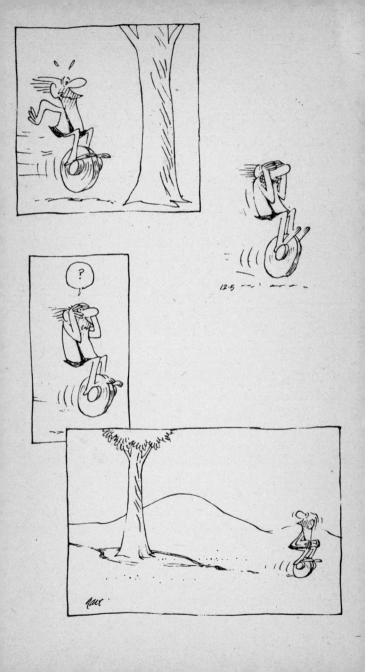

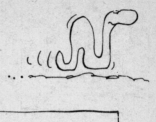

12·7

12.10

DING!

I SUPPOSE YOU'RE WAITING FOR SOME SORT OF A DARN KEWPIE DOLL.....

HELLO?.....

KNOCK KNOCK

GIFTS

12-16

HI THERE,...I AM AN APTERCLAUS. ...A WINGLESS TOYMONGER WITH BATTERIES NOT INCLUDED!

GIFTS

ZIP

WITH ANY LUCK, MY CREDIT CLAM HAS EXPIRED.

GIFTS

12·21

12-23

CL
IN
K

R.I.P

1.5

1·6

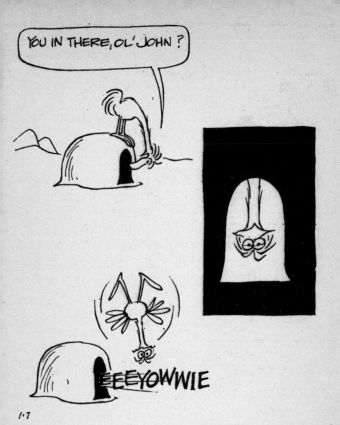

1·7

1.9

bakers dozen

12 of today's cookies

1·12

and one of yesterday's.

hart

HOW CUTE, ...A ONE-LEGGED SNOWMAN.

1-15

AAARRRGGHHHHH

1.19

I'VE BEEN GETTING COMPLAINTS FROM SEVERAL OF OUR SUBSCRIBERS.... SEEMS THEY'VE BEEN GETTING LATE DELIVERIES!

EDITOR

1·29

.. I WANT YOU TO GET TO THE BOTTOM OF THIS!

RIGHT, CHIEF, I'LL......✳

EXTRA, EXTRA,...READ ALL ABOUT IT! "GOD CREATES THE HEAVEN AND THE EARTH!"

Dear Fat Broad,
      How do I get rid
of a Latin lover?....

2:3

He's tall and dark
and very groovy but
I dig short dumpy
guys.

          perplexed.

WHERE
'YOU GOING?

EDITOR

I'VE GOT A
HOUSE CALL.

Hart

2-8

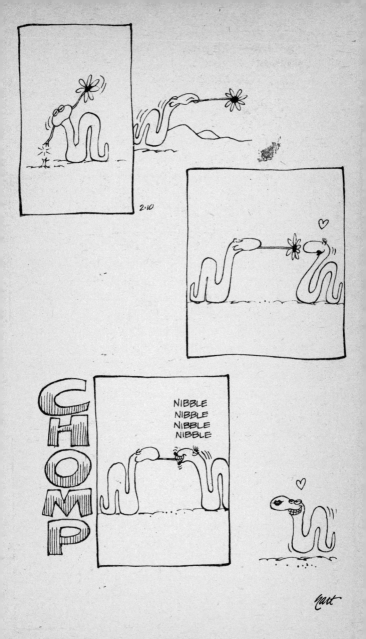

2-11

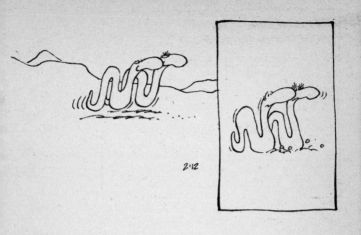

2·12

2·16

 2:20

2-22

2-23

3-24

226

37

3-4

SWISH

LOVE FORTY!

3·5

THE GREAT 'SPORTS OVERLAP' IS DRIVING ME NUTS !

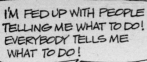

3.15

PATRIOTISM! ...THAT'S WHAT THIS COUNTRY LACKS!

WE MUST HOLD DEAR THE PRINCIPLES OF FREEDOM, EQUALITY, JUSTICE AND STUFF LIKE THAT!

3·16

WHERE IS OUR NATIONAL PRIDE?

SOMEHOW I CAN'T PICTURE NEIL SAYING: "THE DOOKEY BIRD HAS LANDED."

3·17

3·18

3·24

3·31

I'M SATISFIED WITH MY FIGURE.

IN THIS JOB ONE DEALS WITH A LOT OF PATHOS.

4.2

49

4·10

ZOT

4.17

RAAAHHHHH

4.24

.....SO THEN KING NEPTUNE MARRIED THE LOVELY MERMAID, AND THEY LIVED HAPPILY EVER AFTER.

4·30

5·16

5-11

5·20

FORK
IN
ROAD

BLUMP

5-21

5·22

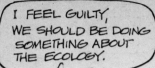

6-1

6-2 hart

GIMMIE A TICKET TO NEXT WEEK'S EARTHQUAKE.

6·14

WHERE WOULD YOU LIKE TO SIT?

TICKETS

YOU GOT ANYTHING NEAR THE EXIT?

TICKETS

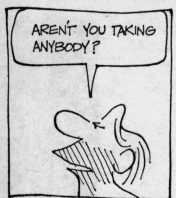

FAWCETT GOLD MEDAL BOOKS
in the B.C. series by Johnny Hart include:

Buy them at your local bookstores or use this handy coupon for ordering:

FAWCETT BOOKS GROUP
P.O. Box C730, 524 Myrtle Ave., Pratt Station, Brooklyn, N.Y. 11205

Please send me the books I have checked above. Orders for less than 5 books must include 75¢ for the first book and 25¢ for each additional book to cover mailing and handling. I enclose $_____ in check or money order.

Name_____

Address_____

City_____State/Zip_____

Please allow 4 to 5 weeks for delivery.